THE GOSPEL
OF THOMAS

A New Translation
for Spiritual Seekers

>>>>>>>>>>>>>>>>>>>>>>>

THE GOSPEL
OF THOMAS

A New Translation
for Spiritual Seekers

by Mark M. Mattison

First Edition

Contents

Acknowledgements

I'd like to express my gratitude to all the women and men of the Grand Rapids Writer's Exchange who have played such an important role in my journey as a writer over the last eight years. Their constructive criticism of my writing has been invaluable.

Particular thanks are due to those writers and readers who commented on the entire manuscript: Daniel June, David Hewitt, Isabella Riley, Terri Lindberg, Wayne Nelson, and Wes Thompson.

Most of all, I'm deeply grateful to my wife, Rebecca, whose graceful and patient encouragement is a source of inexhaustible spiritual strength.

Introduction

The four Gospels of the New Testament – Mathew, Mark, Luke, and John – are well-known and familiar to Christians worldwide. The first three – Matthew, Mark, and Luke – are so similar that they're commonly described as "the Synoptic Gospels." The fourth one, John, is less like the other three, but similar enough in broad outline to complement the others.

Many read these Gospels regularly – for Bible studies, for Sunday School classes, for Sunday morning worship. These four Gospels are part of the "canon" (standard) of twenty-seven books that make up the universally recognized New Testament of traditional churches. We study them to learn what Jesus said and did and what that means for us today. But are these the only Gospels?

What if archaeologists were to discover another one? What if another Gospel were to be unearthed from the sands of the Middle East? Would that add to our understanding of Jesus? Would we need to add another book to our traditional Bibles? These are not simply academic questions. Remarkably, this is exactly what has happened – another Gospel about Jesus, long thought to have been lost, has been rediscovered within the last hundred years.

Up until about a hundred years ago, we knew about this Gospel only through the writings of the so-called "Church Fathers." Early in the third century, both Hippolytus and Origen referred to it. But the Gospel itself did not appear to have survived.

Near the end of the nineteenth century, however, some Greek fragments of a previously unknown Gospel were uncovered by archaeologists in Egypt. These three papyri fragments were first published in 1897. But it wasn't until 1945 that a complete copy was discovered near Nag Hammadi in Egypt. This one was written in Coptic, the ancient Egyptian language written in Greek letters, commonly used from about 300 to 1000 CE.[1] Only after that discovery did scholars realize that the earlier Greek papyri were really fragments of the long-lost Gospel of Thomas.

Scholars have since debated the meaning and significance of this monumental discovery. Though other Gospels were also discovered at Nag Hammadi (like the Gospel of Philip and the Gospel of Truth), and other Gospels have since come to light (like the Gospel of Mary and the Gospel of Judas), the Gospel of Thomas remains the most well-known and controversial of all the non-canonical Gospels. What does this newly-recovered Gospel say, and what does it really mean?

The most obvious question to consider first is who Thomas was. Unfortunately, very little is actually said about the Apostle Thomas in our earliest texts. The New Testament Gospels list him among the twelve disciples,[2] and only John describes him actually doing or saying anything.[3] John provides one additional detail, describing him as "the one called Didymos."[4] The Greek name "Didymos" and the Semitic name "Thomas" both mean "Twin." Significantly, Thomas' Gospel describes him as "Didymos Judas Thomas" in the opening sentence, so the identification with the Thomas of the New Testament Gospels seems clear.

As we'll see in the following chapters, however, this Gospel wasn't actually written by Thomas, but rather in a tradition traced to Thomas. This tradition is not limited to Thomas' Gospel; for example, another early text, the Syrian Acts of Thomas, also describes him as "Didymos Judas Thomas." According to this account, Thomas was Jesus' twin brother, sent to India to spread Jesus' message. Though the Acts of Thomas is clearly legendary, it does preserve the ancient tradition that Thomas was the Apostle to the East, providing a plausible context for the nature of the Gospel that bears his name.

In the chapters that follow, we'll consider not only the most widespread scholarly opinions about the Gospel of Thomas, we'll also consider what it promises for contemporary spiritual seekers. Though this book isn't intended for scholars – and though many scholars will undoubtedly question this approach – nevertheless it is my sincere hope that the approach suggested here may help to bridge the gap between historical academic research and contemporary spiritual concerns. With that in mind, we may begin with an overview of the principal opinions about the Gospel of Thomas.

1
The Debate about Thomas' Gospel

Though the available literature about Thomas' Gospel is far too voluminous to be documented in this brief book, much of it can be divided into two clearly defined camps. Evangelical scholars tend to argue for a late (second-century) date of Thomas, claiming that it is based on the canonical Gospels (Matthew, Mark, Luke, and John) – making it easier to dismiss it as a "heretical" deviation of historic Christianity.[1] By contrast, other scholars tend to argue for an early (first-century) date of Thomas, claiming that it represents a less dogmatic, more original form of Christianity free of the judgmental and doctrinal constraints of a later "orthodoxy."

Simply put, the debate over the dating and interpretation of Thomas' Gospel has become a proxy for a broader debate about the legitimacy of the institutional church today.

These two opposing viewpoints can be illustrated by select citations from popular scholars who share the same assumptions about the incompatibility of Thomas' theology with that of the canonical New Testament. Representing the early-date view, Harold Bloom writes that unlike the New Testament Gospels, Thomas:

> spares us the crucifixion, makes the resurrection unnecessary, and does not present us with a God named Jesus. No dogmas could be founded upon this sequence (if it is a sequence) of apothegms. If you turn to the Gospel of Thomas, you encounter a Jesus who is unsponsored and free. No one could be burned or even scorned in the name of this Jesus, and no one has been hurt in anyway, except perhaps for those

bigots, high church or low, who may have glanced at so permanently surprising a work.[2]

However, Thomas does describe both the cross (cf. Saying 55) and resurrection (cf. Saying 5) and doesn't hesitate to denounce sin and evil (cf. Saying 45) – suggesting that Bloom's description of an easygoing Jesus is based on a somewhat selective reading of the Gospel. Similarly, in her book *Beyond Belief: The Secret Gospel of Thomas*, Elaine Pagels sketches out a theology of Thomas based on only 17 sayings – about fifteen percent of the total.[3]

On the evangelical side, James D.G. Dunn presupposes the same incompatibility when he writes that "The *Thomas* material which parallels the Synoptic tradition lacks the distinctive message of *Thomas*,"[4] that "it is hard to see the distinctive *Thomas* message as drawn from the Jesus tradition as attested in the Synoptic (and the Johannine) Gospels,"[5] and "The basic narrative of *Thomas* is too distinctive and too different from the other first century indications of the impact made by Jesus for us to find a root for the *Thomas* perspective in Jesus' mission or the early oral Jesus tradition."[6] Again, the focus seems to be on the material unique to Thomas' Gospel, quite apart from the book in its entirety.

What drives the mutual assumption of both sides that Thomas is fundamentally incompatible with the canonical Gospels? Approximately half of Jesus' sayings in Thomas are already familiar to us from the canonical New Testament Gospels. Scholars on both sides of the divide seem to focus on the portions of Thomas that are unique to Thomas' Gospel, developing interpretations that place it in opposition to historic Christianity.

Another well-known evangelical scholar, N.T. Wright, has been known to quip that "the so-called 'Gospel of Thomas' … is in fact not a Gospel and not by Thomas."[7] Unfortunately, this is one of those instances when Wright's witty talent for memorable prose gets the better of him, for at least two reasons.

First, the Coptic manuscript of Thomas actually titles it a "Gospel," so to argue otherwise seems like contemporary hubris. We may certainly disagree with this Gospel in whole or in part, but it's difficult to understand how anyone can justifiably deny that it's a type of literature that it unambiguously presents itself to be.[8]

Second, Wright actually agrees with most biblical scholars that we don't really know who wrote any of the Gospels. For instance, in the same book, he writes that:

> We don't know whether Luke really was, as is often thought, the companion of Paul. We don't know whether the 'Beloved Disciple', to whom the Fourth Gospel is ascribed (John 21:24), was really 'John' (in which case, which 'John'?) or someone else. None of the books name their authors; all the traditions about who wrote which ones are just that, traditions, from later on in the life of the church (beginning in the first half of the second century, about fifty years after the Gospels were written).[9]

Consequently, the fact that we don't really know who wrote Thomas' Gospel is simply not a relevant consideration.

Though Wright believes Thomas "far more likely ... represents a radical translation, and indeed subversion, of first-century Christianity into a quite different sort of religion," that it "reflects a symbolic universe, and a worldview, which are radically different to those of ... early Judaism and Christianity"[10] and "that some of the sayings in *Thomas* are derived from the synoptic tradition," he also admits that "some, which may well go back a very long way, are independent."[11]

In spite of that reluctant admission, however, Wright perpetuates the consensus on both sides when he argues that if "we take the ahistorical route pioneered by *Thomas,* we are left in a world of private dualistic piety."[12] His point is that Thomas represents an internalized spirituality incompatible with what he believes is the earlier and more authentic spirituality of the canonical Gospels.

However, it can easily be argued that Thomas' Gospel is just as concerned about concrete historical issues and social justice as any of the canonical Gospels. For instance, like Matthew 5:3 and Luke 6:20, in Thomas Jesus says "Blessed are those who are poor, for yours is the kingdom of heaven" (Saying 54, literal translation). Similarly, as in Matthew 5:42 and Luke 6:30,34-35, in Thomas Jesus says "If you have money, don't lend it at interest. Instead, give it to someone from whom you won't get it back" (Saying 95; cf. also Sayings 63 and 69). And on at least one occasion, Thomas' Gospel arguably surpasses the canonical Gospels in condemning economic exploitation in the Parable of the Dinner Party when it criticizes those "who are consumed with buying and selling" (Saying 64). So the claim that Thomas' Gospel presents a perspective diametrically opposed to the concrete social concerns of the canonical Gospels is weaker than it may initially seem.

Is it possible that scholars on both sides of this debate have overstated the issues in their haste to defend or undermine historic Christianity? Is it possible to articulate a middle path, an approach that takes Thomas' Gospel seriously on its own terms, irrespective of one's level of comfort with the institutional church? Put differently, can Thomas' Gospel be read on its own merits, or even alongside more traditional Gospels? I believe the answer to all these questions is an unqualified "Yes." The comments of the French Orthodox theologian Jean Yves-Leloup on this point are worth quoting at length:

> Is the Yeshua [Jesus] of Thomas different from the Yeshua of the other gospels? Undoubtedly! But this difference resides not so much in the ultimate nature of the Christ as in the presentation of his teaching. It is a difference of hearing, rather than of words. Thus it is possible to read this gospel in a Catholic, Orthodox, or other manner, just as we read Luke, Mark, Matthew, and John in different ways.

There is no need to enter into a dualistic polemic, setting the Gospel of Thomas against the canonical gospels, considering it superior to them and the only authentic gospel. To do so would, after all, be merely to give in to a reaction against the other dualistic polemic that has branded the Thomas Gospel as a fabrication of lies and heresies. ...

Might it not be that our task is to read all the gospels *together,* seeing them as different points of view of the Christ, different points of view that exist both within us and outside of us, in historical and meta-historical dimensions? Does not the Nag Hammadi discovery, with this sublime jewel of a gospel, reveal to us new facets of the unchanging Eternal Jewel? Is it not our task to go beyond both naïve enthusiasm and doctrinaire suspicion to cultivate the ear of the golden mean and to learn to listen to the Spirit, which speaks to all human beings, beyond all Churches, religions, and elites?[13]

The position taken here is that Thomas doesn't represent a threat to historic Christianity (for better or for worse), but rather a potentially deeper and broader appreciation for what Christianity has to offer. Scholars have long recognized that different Gospels offer unique perspectives, but these different perspectives shed light on different aspects of Christian reflections about Jesus, his teachings, and his ministry. Some, like Matthew and Luke, speak to church organization (among other things), whereas others, like John, Mary, and Thomas often focus on more inner spiritual concerns. That's not to say, of course, that Matthew and Luke are unconcerned about inner spirituality, nor that John, Mary, and Thomas are unconcerned about social issues; only that their focus is different.

All Gospels have their place. The canonical Gospels never claimed to have the last word – the four Gospels of the New Testament end with the words: "Jesus did many other things too. If they were all written down, I don't think there'd be enough room in the whole world for all the books that would be written" (John 21:25, DFV).[14]

From this viewpoint, the question of whether the "canon" of traditional Scripture should be revised to include some of these recently-recovered Gospels is not as pressing an issue as it may initially seem. Formal recognition of Scriptures is a question for organized churches, which operate with their own respective models of authority. Consequently, the perspectives reflected in this book may be considered separately from that more involved question.[15]

2

A Collection of Sayings

The previous chapter argued that, taken on its own terms, Thomas' Gospel can be considered as complementary to the canonical Gospels of Matthew, Mark, Luke, and John, and even other Gospels as well (such as Mary's Gospel). Despite the many similarities and parallels, however, Thomas' Gospel lacks the narrative structure so familiar from other Gospels. Instead of presenting a linear storyline, Thomas' Gospel lists 114 sayings of Jesus in no obvious order. To make it even more puzzling, some of the sayings almost seem to be out of order. For example, in Saying 6, Jesus' disciples pose questions to him, questions that he doesn't appear to answer directly until Saying 14.

On the other hand, biblical scholars have long suspected that such sayings lists were commonly circulated among early Christians. This theory is based in part on a comparison of the canonical Gospels themselves.

When comparing the four canonical Gospels, scholars note the uniqueness of John's Gospel, whose content resembles the other three only about eight percent of the time; that is, about 92% of John's Gospel is unique to John. However, the first three canonical Gospels – Matthew, Mark, and Luke – are often referred to collectively as "the Synoptic Gospels" since their contents frequently overlap, often word-for-word. This is usually accounted for by the theory that Mark's Gospel was written first, and that the authors of Matthew and Luke independently copied and edited large portions of Mark's Gospel. However, that leaves about 200 verses that appear in both Matthew and Luke but not in Mark – almost all of them sayings of Jesus.

If the parallels between Matthew, Mark, and Luke can be explained by the dependence of Matthew and Luke on Mark, how can we explain the parallels between Matthew and Luke that don't appear in Mark? The most plausible suggestion is that in addition to Mark's Gospel, Matthew and Luke used another common source, now lost to us, which was comprised simply of a list of Jesus sayings. Scholars have dubbed this hypothetical sayings source "Q," from the German word *quelle* or "source."

Prior to the discovery of Thomas' Gospel, the idea of a list of Jesus sayings was only theoretical. However, Thomas' Gospel appears to be exactly the sort of Gospel that Q is believed to have been – a collection of free-floating Jesus sayings, remnants of an oral tradition preserved by Jesus' earliest followers and passed down from one generation to the next.

Some have taken this as an argument that Thomas' Gospel is earlier than the canonical Gospels,[1] but it's difficult to argue that with any certainty. Even if Thomas were the sort of Gospel that an earlier source of Matthew and Luke was believed to have been, it could still have been written later than the others. It's even possible that Thomas was written at about the same time as the other Gospels and independently of them, committing to writing some of the same oral traditions and memories of Jesus' sayings.[2]

The exact dating of Thomas, and the exact relationship between Thomas and the canonical Gospels, may never be determined with absolute certainty.

Fortunately, however, it is possible to bracket these issues and articulate a broad consensus. Like the canonical Gospels, Thomas' Gospel is widely believed to have been written in Syria in the late first century or the early second century. Like the other Gospels, it also appears to have gone through multiple levels of editing and revisions. The differences between the third-century Greek fragments and the fourth-century Coptic text definitely suggest that different versions were copied over time. Whether the first author of Thomas' Gospel knew the other Gospels, or whether the first authors of the other Gospels knew Thomas' Gospel, is still hotly debated. But regardless of their exact literary relationship, all these early Gospels seem to share some common origins.

Like the Synoptic Gospels, Thomas' Gospel contains many parables and sayings about "the kingdom of heaven" (rendered as "Ultimate Reality" in the colloquial translation of Chapter Four). But like John's Gospel, Thomas' Gospel contains many sayings about light, life, and similar themes. So in many ways Thomas appears as a type of "bridge" between the Synoptic Gospels and John – a fascinating new discovery to help fill in some of the "gaps" of the familiar Gospel record.

Some of the unfamiliar sayings contained in this collection may seem puzzling. This is not only due to the lack of a narrative context, but also to the nature of the sayings themselves. A quick read of these texts in a single setting may provide a broad overview of the Gospel, but as the opening sentences make clear, the meanings are intended to be sought after through intentional contemplation and careful meditation. This is a Gospel of Wisdom sayings, not narrative stories.

The text presented in Chapter Four is a fresh translation intended to present Thomas' Gospel in easy-to-read, colloquial English. It is not, strictly speaking, a literal translation of the Coptic original.

The translation philosophy is similar to that of many contemporary Bible translations. Known as "dynamic equivalence" (as opposed to "formal equivalence"), it seeks to convey the basic idea of the original language even if it means diverging somewhat from the exact verbiage of the original.

More literal translations are readily available from other sources. However, none of those more literal translations are available in the public domain. Consequently, and also in order to "balance out" the colloquial translation, a more literal translation of the original Coptic text has been developed for the Appendix of this book. The translation in the Appendix is being committed to the public domain and may be freely copied and used for any purpose.

Chapter Three provides a more detailed explanation of the differences between these two versions.

3
About These Translations

The fresh new translation of Thomas' Gospel in Chapter Four differs somewhat from the more literal public domain translation that follows in the Appendix. Chapter Two described the differences in terms of "dynamic equivalence" and "formal equivalence." Though the two versions are very similar in most respects, some brief explanations of the differences are in order. Why two different versions?

One reason is that the more "free" or "loose" translation incorporates the third-century Greek fragments. In other words, the more complete Coptic text of the fourth century has been supplemented with parallel sayings from the earlier Greek texts which contain additional content not present in the Coptic. That explains the differences between Sayings 2, 5, and 36 in these two translations. The difference in Saying 5 is particularly noteworthy since this is the only saying in Thomas that mentions resurrection; that part of the text is not preserved in the later Coptic. The more "literal" translation of the Appendix is based only on the later Coptic text, without reference to the Greek.

Similarly, the more "free" translation of Saying 93 fills in the "gaps" of the text by comparison with Matthew's Gospel, whereas the more "literal" translation from the Coptic contains ellipses showing the gap in the existing manuscript. In general, words reconstructed based on the size of the gaps are contained in brackets in the Appendix, with ellipses representing gaps where reconstruction is more difficult.

Other differences are rhetorical, with the more "free" version avoiding technical religious jargon. For instance, the more "literal" translation in the Appendix uses the word "blasphemy" in Saying 44 whereas the more "free" translation uses the less "religious" term "slander," and where the more "literal" translation uses the term "persecution," the more "free" translation uses the term "harassment" in Sayings 68 and 69. Similarly, where the more "literal" translation uses the word "yoke" in Saying 90, the more "free" translation uses the word "work."

Both translations use various strategies to avoid the masculine generic (such as "fisher" instead of "fisherman" in Saying 8 and "human" or "person" instead of "man" throughout), but the "free" version occasionally takes an extra step in that direction (such as adding the word "sisters" alongside "brothers" in Saying 99).

The remaining differences in translation are philosophical. For example, Sayings 55 and 101 in the more "free" translation use the word "disregard" instead of "hate":

Jesus said, "Whoever doesn't *disregard* their father and mother can't become my disciple, and whoever doesn't *disregard* their brothers and sisters and take up their cross like I do isn't worthy of me" (Saying 55, A New Translation)

Jesus said, "Whoever doesn't *hate* their father and mother can't become my disciple, and whoever doesn't *hate* their brothers and sisters and take up their cross like I do isn't worthy of me" (Saying 55, A Literal Translation)

"Whoever doesn't *disregard* their father and mother as I do can't become my disciple" (Saying 101, A New Translation)

"Whoever doesn't *hate* their [father] and mother as I do can't become my [disciple]" (Saying 101, A Literal Translation)

The difference reflects the figurative meaning of the word "hate" in its original cultural context, in which an overstatement intends to convey fact that "even natural affection for our loved ones dare not interfere or take precedence over loyalty to him" (or his teaching).[1] Although the Coptic word literally means "to hate" in these sayings (as reflected in the Appendix), that more literal translation does not necessarily reflect the original intent of the saying.

A more significant difference can be seen in ten Sayings[2] where the more "literal" translation uses the word "Father," and in Sayings 3 and 50, where it uses the term "living Father." In a gender-neutral translation, there are no obvious strategies for addressing masculine terminology for the Divine in the original text. Describing "God" as "Father" not only privileges masculine language over feminine language, it also limits our understanding of all that God truly is, which transcends rational conception.

Many people's idea of "God" is an artificial construct, a "bigger and better" image of ourselves. "God" is described with lofty terms like "omnipotent," "omniscient," and "omnipresent" – essentially, a limitless divine "Being" – but still essentially conceived as an independent personality, an "intelligent designer" or "grand master" who presides over "his" creation, quite apart from it and also subject to very human-like emotions, attributes, and motivations. This "God" is like a wise old man on a throne passing judgment from a distant heaven, a "creator" or "builder" brooding over "his" creation the way a child may oversee a Lego structure to be developed, altered, or dismantled.

In the mystical tradition, however, "God" is often conceived in "transpersonal" terms. That is, we may experience "God" as a personal presence, but "God" is *more* than personal; "God" transcends personal existence. "God" is not a limited personality overseeing "his" or "her" creation, but a transcendent divine reality permeating all things. In John 4:24, Jesus describes "God" as "spirit," and in John 3:8 Jesus describes this divine reality in mysterious terms: "The wind blows where it wants to, and you hear its sound, but you don't know where it comes from or where it's going" (DFV). Similarly, in Acts 17, we read of the Divine in whom "we live, and move, and exist" (v. 28, DFV), and that "we shouldn't think that the Divine can be compared to … an image formed by human skill and imagination" (v. 29, DFV). Words like "Father" are mere metaphors (and very limiting metaphors at that) for this divine reality, this ultimate ground of all existence. All of creation, both visible and invisible, is grounded in this divine Source, which exists in and through all things.

In Saying 77, Jesus speaks as the incarnate Divine Word. "Split a log," he says, and "I'm there. Lift the stone, and you'll find me there." Though this may sound like the doctrine of "pantheism" (i.e., all things collectively make up "God"), note that Jesus or "God" aren't actually *identified* with logs and stones. The idea is closer to "panentheism," the doctrine that all things exist *in* "God" (cf. Ephesians 1:23).[3] All of creation (seen and unseen) is an extension of divine reality, reaching out in a profound act of self-discovery ("everything" comes "from me and unfolds toward me," Thomas Saying 77). The idea is that the Divine doesn't exist as an independent conscious "Supreme Being" so much as an unfolding reality inextricably bound up with (and expanding in) all of creation, vividly described as invisible "wind" in John 3:8. The Book of Revelation uses the language of "the first and the last" and "the alpha and the omega,"[4] the beginning and the end, which resonates deeply with Saying 18 in Thomas' Gospel.

In order to reflect this more sublime concept of the Divine, the more "free" translation of Thomas uses the word "Source" instead of "Father." This term is not only suitable as a more expansive way of describing "God," but also useful as a generic term which encompasses the more limited term "Father," among other ways of describing "God." So although this rather free translation choice moves further from the literal text of Thomas, it does approximate Thomas' meaning.

Another important difference involves the terms "the kingdom," "the kingdom of heaven," "my Father's kingdom," and "the places of my Father" which appear in a total of nineteen Sayings in the more "literal" translation.[5] The term "kingdom" is just as problematic in our contemporary context, especially given its imperial connotations. Compounding the problem is the obvious fact that "the kingdom" is clearly a figure of speech in Thomas' Gospel and elsewhere, although what this figure of speech signifies is nowhere explained in any Gospel. "The kingdom" is frequently illustrated and described, but nowhere defined, which in itself is illuminating. If the Gospels never attempt to define exactly what "the kingdom" is, perhaps we need to be circumspect.

What, then, may we say "the kingdom" is? What we can say with certainty is that in Thomas' Gospel, "the kingdom" is something internal (Saying 3); as in the Synoptic Gospels, it's something to be compared to using various similes;[6] it's something to be "entered" (Sayings 22, 99, 114); something to be "found" (Sayings 27, 49, 54, and 82); and, finally, something to be "known" (Sayings 46 and 113).

From all this it's clear that "the kingdom" is not a literal nation-state like a "theocracy" or a restored Davidic kingdom, but rather something accessible in the here-and-now. In her book *The Wisdom Jesus*, Cynthia Bourgeault follows Jim Marion in describing "the Kingdom of Heaven" as "a state of consciousness." She defines it as "nondual consciousness" or "unitive consciousness."[7]

Though I don't disagree – and those terms are all consistent with the Sayings cited above – nevertheless in the more "free" translation I've chosen to render this term as "Ultimate Reality," a term which not only encompasses the idea of "unitive" or "cosmic consciousness" but is perhaps less likely to be conceived in equally limited terms as a personal state of mind rather than a cosmic reality that also transcends easily categorized definitions.

It is in this mystical context that we should consider another key term in Thomas' Gospel, one that is often translated as "alone" or "solitary," usually with the implication that it refers to celibacy. That term is the Greek word *monachos*, which is used in the Coptic translation of Thomas in three places: Sayings 16, 49, and 75. However, other meanings are equally plausible in the context of Thomas. For example, in her article "The Origins and Idiosyncrasies of the Earliest Form of Asceticism," Gabriele

Winkler writes: "It seems that the Greek word *monachos* derives from the Syriac *ihidaya*, as Adam has tried to demonstrate: *monachos* is the Greek translation of the older Syriac *ihidaya*."[8] As for the meaning of *ihidaya*, Winkler writes that in addition to "'single one' ... it can also refer to someone who is single-minded, including the broader associations of 'being one' or 'unified.'"[9] On this basis, the translations of Thomas presented here translate the term simply as "One,"[10] implying the achievement of nondual or unitive consciousness, that is, spiritual enlightenment.[11]

One other controversial translation strategy is worth mentioning: The choice of the word "courageous" instead of "male" in Saying 114 (or even "manly," as in the more "literal" translation). This is the scandalous text in which Peter criticizes Mary Magdalene on the basis that "women aren't worthy of life," to which Jesus responds (in most translations) by saying that "every woman who makes herself male will enter the kingdom of heaven."

The translation choice here of "courageous" instead of "male" is based on the philological argument described by Samuel Zinner,[12] building on the argument of Paul Schüngel.[13] This is Zinner's translation of Saying 114:

> Simon Peter said to them: "Let Mary depart from among us, for women are not worthy of Life." Jesus said: "Look, am I to force her to become male? In order that she also may become a living spirit, her spirit is equal to that of you males. For every woman who will make herself *capable* will enter the kingdom of heaven (emphasis mine).

Again, although the Coptic word which Zinner renders as "capable" literally means "male," Zinner agrees with Schüngel's argument that "capable," "worthy," or "fit" is fully within the range of semantic meanings,[14] even though that in turn rests on a patriarchal assumption of what it means to be "manly." This rhetorical approach to Saying 114 is more consistent with

Thomas' emphasis elsewhere on "male" and "female" becoming One, as in Saying 22 (cp. Galatians 3:28).

Apart from the issues described in this chapter, the translation of Chapter Four is similar to the translation in the Appendix which is based only on the fourth-century Coptic text of Thomas' Gospel.

4
The Gospel of Thomas
A New Translation

Introduction

These are the hidden sayings that the living Jesus spoke and Didymos Judas Thomas wrote down.

Saying One:
True Meaning

And he said, "Whoever discovers the meaning of these sayings won't taste death."

Saying Two:
Seek and Find

Jesus said, "Whoever seeks shouldn't stop until they find. When they find, they'll be disturbed. When they're disturbed, they'll be amazed, and reign over everything. When they've reigned, then they'll rest."

Saying Three:
Seeking Within

Jesus said, "If your leaders tell you, 'Look, Ultimate Reality is in heaven,' then the birds of heaven will precede you. If they tell you, 'It's in the sea,' then the fish will precede you. Rather, Ultimate Reality is within you and outside of you.

"When you know yourselves, then you'll be known, and you'll realize that you're the children of the living Source. But if you don't know yourselves, then you live in poverty, and you are the poverty."

Saying Four:
First and Last

Jesus said, "The older person won't hesitate to ask a little seven-day-old child about the place of life, and they'll live, because many who are first will be last, and they'll become One."

Saying Five:
Hidden and Revealed

Jesus said, "Know what's in front of your face, and what's hidden from you will be revealed to you, because there's nothing hidden that won't be revealed, and nothing buried that won't be raised."

Saying Six:
Public Ritual

His disciples asked him, "Do you want us to fast? And how should we pray? Should we make donations? And what food should we avoid?"

Jesus said, "Don't lie, and don't do what you hate, because everything is revealed in the sight of heaven; for there's nothing hidden that won't be revealed, and nothing covered up that will stay secret."

Saying Seven:
The Lion and the Human

Jesus said, "Blessed is the lion that's eaten by a human and then becomes human, but how awful for the human who's eaten by a lion, and the lion becomes human."

Saying Eight:
The Parable of the Fish

He said, "The human being is like a wise fisher who cast a net into the sea and drew it up from the sea full of little fish. Among them the wise fisher found a fine large fish and cast all the little fish back down into the sea, easily choosing the large fish. Anyone who has ears to hear should hear!"

Saying Nine:
The Parable of the Sower

Jesus said, "Look, a sower went out, took a handful of seeds, and scattered them. Some fell on the roadside; the birds came and gathered them. Others fell on the rock; they didn't take root in the soil and ears of grain didn't rise toward heaven. Yet others fell on thorns; they choked the seeds and worms ate them. Finally, others fell on good soil; it produced fruit up toward heaven, some sixty times as much and some a hundred and twenty."

Saying Ten:
Jesus and Fire (1)

Jesus said, "I've cast fire on the world, and look, I'm watching over it until it blazes."

Saying Eleven:
Those Who Are Living Won't Die (1)

Jesus said, "This heaven will disappear, and the one above it will disappear too. Those who are dead aren't alive, and those who are living won't die. In the days when you ate what was dead, you made it alive. When you're in the light, what will you do? On the day when you were One, you became divided. But when you become divided, what will you do?"

Saying Twelve:
James the Just

"We know you're going to leave us," the disciples told Jesus. "Who will lead us then?"

Jesus told them, "Wherever you are, you'll go to James the Just, for whom heaven and earth came into being."

Saying Thirteen:
Thomas' Confession

Jesus asked his disciples, "If you were to compare me to someone, who would you say I'm like?"

Simon Peter told him, "You're like a just angel."

Matthew told him, "You're like a wise philosopher."

Thomas told him, "Teacher, I'm completely unable to say whom you're like."

"I'm not your teacher," Jesus said. "Because you've drunk, you've become intoxicated by the bubbling spring I've measured out."

He took him aside and told him three things. When Thomas returned to his companions, they asked, "What did Jesus say to you?"

"If I tell you one of the things he said to me," Thomas told them, "you'll pick up stones and cast them at me, and fire will come out of the stones and burn you up."

Saying Fourteen:
Public Ministry

Jesus told them, "If you fast, you'll bring guilt upon yourselves; and if you pray, you'll be condemned; and if you make donations, you'll harm your spirits.

"If they welcome you when you enter any land and go around in the countryside, heal those who are sick among them and eat whatever they give you, because it's not what goes into your mouth that will defile you. What comes out of your mouth is what will defile you."

Saying Fifteen:
Worship

Jesus said, "When you see the one who wasn't born of a woman, fall down on your face and worship that person. That's your Source."

Saying Sixteen:
Not Peace, but War

Jesus said, "Maybe people think that I've come to cast peace on the world, and they don't know that I've come to cast divisions on the earth: fire, sword, and war. Where there are five in a house, there'll be three against two and two against three, father against and son and son against father. They'll stand up and be One."

Saying Seventeen:
Divine Gift

Jesus said, "I'll give you what no eye has ever seen, no ear has ever heard, no hand has ever touched, and no human mind has ever thought."

Saying Eighteen:
Beginning and End

The disciples asked Jesus, "Tell us about our end. How will it come?"

Jesus asked, "Have you discovered the beginning so that you can look for the end? Because the end will be where the beginning is. Blessed is the one who will stand up in the beginning. They'll know the end, and won't taste death."

Saying Nineteen:
Five Trees in Paradise

Jesus said, "Blessed is the one who came into being before coming into being. If you become my disciples and listen to my message, these stones will become your servants; because there are five trees in paradise which don't change in summer or winter, and their leaves don't fall. Whoever knows them won't taste death."

Saying Twenty:
The Parable of the Mustard Seed

The disciples asked Jesus, "Tell us, what can Ultimate Reality be compared to?"

He told them, "It can be compared to a mustard seed. Though it's the smallest of all the seeds, when it falls on tilled soil it makes a plant so large that it shelters the birds of heaven."

Saying Twenty-One:
The Parables of the Field, the Bandits, and the Reaper

Mary asked Jesus, "Whom are your disciples like?"

"They're like little children living in a field which isn't theirs," he said. "When the owners of the field come, they'll say, 'Give our field back to us.' They'll strip naked in front of them to let them have it and give them their field.

"So I say that if the owner of the house realizes the bandit is coming, they'll watch out beforehand and won't let the bandit break into the house of their domain and steal their possessions. You, then, watch out for the world! Prepare to defend yourself so that the bandits don't attack you, because what you're expecting will come. May there be a wise person among you!

"When the fruit ripened, the reaper came quickly, sickle in hand, and harvested it. Anyone who has ears to hear should hear!"

Saying Twenty-Two:
Making the Two into One

Jesus saw some little children nursing. "These nursing children," he told his disciples, "can be compared to those who enter Ultimate Reality."

They asked him, "Then we'll enter Ultimate Reality as little children?"

"When you make the two into One," Jesus told them, "and make the inner like the outer and the outer like the inner, and the upper like the lower, and so make the male and the female a single One so that the male won't be male nor the female female; when you make eyes in the place of an eye, a hand in the place of a hand, a foot in the place of a foot, and an image in the place of an image; then you'll enter Ultimate Reality."

Saying Twenty-Three:
Those Who are Chosen (1)

Jesus said, "I'll choose you, one out of a thousand and two out of ten thousand, and they'll stand as a single One."

Saying Twenty-Four:
Light

"Show us the place where you are," his disciples said, "because we need to look for it."

"Anyone who has ears to hear should hear!" he told them. "Light exists within people of light, and they light up the whole world. If they don't shine, there's darkness."

Saying Twenty-Five:
Love and Protect

Jesus said, "Love your brother or sister as your own soul. Protect them like the pupil of your eye."

Saying Twenty-Six:
Speck and Beam

Jesus said, "You see the speck that's in your brother's or sister's eye, but you don't see the beam in your own eye. When you get the beam out of your own eye, then you'll be able to see clearly to get the speck out of your brother's or sister's eye."

Saying Twenty-Seven:
Fasting and Sabbath

"If you don't fast from the world, you won't find Ultimate Reality. If you don't make the Sabbath into a Sabbath, you won't see the Source."

Saying Twenty-Eight:
The World is Drunk

Jesus said, "I stood in the middle of the world and appeared to them in the flesh. I found them all drunk; I didn't find any of them thirsty. My soul ached for the children of humanity, because they were blind in their hearts and couldn't see. They came into the world empty and plan on leaving the world empty. Meanwhile, they're drunk. When they shake off their wine, then they'll change."

Saying Twenty-Nine:
Spirit and Body

Jesus said, "If the flesh came into existence because of spirit, that's amazing. If spirit came into existence because of the body, that's really amazing! But I'm amazed at how such great wealth has been placed in this poverty."

Saying Thirty:
Divine Presence

Jesus said, "Where there are three deities, they're divine. Where there are two or one, I'm with them."

Saying Thirty-One:
Prophet and Doctor

Jesus said, "No prophet is welcome in their own village. No doctor heals those who know them."

Saying Thirty-Two:
The Parable of the Fortified City

Jesus said, "A city built and fortified on a high mountain can't fall, nor can it be hidden."

Saying Thirty-Three:
The Parable of the Lamp

Jesus said, "What you hear with one ear, listen to with both, then proclaim from your rooftops. No one lights a lamp and puts it under a basket or in a hidden place. Rather, they put it on the stand so that everyone who comes and goes can see its light."

Saying Thirty-Four:
The Parable of Those Who Can't See

Jesus said, "If someone who's blind leads someone else who's blind, both of them fall into a pit."

Saying Thirty-Five:
The Parable of Binding the Strong

Jesus said, "No one can break into the house of the strong and take it by force without first tying the hands of the strong. Then they can loot the house."

Saying Thirty-Six:
Anxiety

Jesus said, "Don't be anxious from morning to evening or from evening to morning about what you'll wear. You're much better than the lilies, which don't work or spin. When you have no clothes, what will you put on? Who can add one moment to your life? That's who will give you your clothes."

Saying Thirty-Seven:
Seeing Jesus

"When will you appear to us?" his disciples asked. "When will we see you?"

"When you strip naked without being ashamed," Jesus said, "and throw your clothes on the ground and stomp on them as little children would, then you'll see the Son of the Living One and won't be afraid."

Saying Thirty-Eight:
Finding Jesus

Jesus said, "Often you've wanted to hear this message that I'm telling you, and you don't have anyone else from whom to hear it. There will be days when you'll look for me, but you won't be able to find me."

Saying Thirty-Nine:
The Keys of Knowledge

Jesus said, "The Pharisees and the scholars have taken the keys of knowledge and hidden them. They haven't entered, and haven't let others enter who wanted to. So be wise as serpents and innocent as doves."

Saying Forty:
A Grapevine

Jesus said, "A grapevine has been planted apart from the Source. Since it's malnourished, it'll be pulled up by its root and destroyed."

Saying Forty-One:
More and Less

Jesus said, "Whoever has something in hand will be given more, but whoever doesn't have anything will lose even what little they do have."

Saying Forty-Two:
Passing By

Jesus said, "Become passersby."

Saying Forty-Three:
The Tree and the Fruit

"Who are you to say these things to us?" his disciples asked him.

"You don't realize who I am from what I say to you, but you've become like those Judeans who either love the tree but hate its fruit, or love the fruit but hate the tree."

Saying Forty-Four:
Slander

Jesus said, "Whoever slanders the Source will be forgiven, and whoever slanders the Son will be forgiven, but whoever slanders the Holy Spirit will not be forgiven, neither on earth nor in heaven."

Saying Forty-Five:
Good and Evil

Jesus said, "Grapes aren't harvested from thorns, nor are figs gathered from thistles, because they don't produce fruit. A person who's good brings good things out of their treasure, and a person who's evil brings evil things out of their evil treasure. They say evil things because their heart is full of evil."

Saying Forty-Six:
Greater than John the Baptizer

Jesus said, "From Adam to John the Baptizer, no one's been born who's so much greater than John the Baptizer that they shouldn't avert their eyes. But I say that whoever among you will become a little child will know Ultimate Reality and become greater than John."

Saying Forty-Seven:
The Parables of Divided Loyalties, New Wine in Old Wineskins, and New Patch on Old Cloth

Jesus said, "It's not possible for anyone to mount two horses or stretch two bows, and it's not possible for a servant to follow two leaders, because they'll respect one and despise the other.

"No one drinks old wine and immediately wants to drink new wine. And new wine isn't put in old wineskins, because they'd burst. Nor is old wine put in new wineskins, because it'd spoil.

"A new patch of cloth isn't sewn onto an old coat, because it'd tear apart."

Saying Forty-Eight:
Unity (1)

Jesus said, "If two make peace with each other in a single house, they'll say to the mountain, 'Go away,' and it will."

Saying Forty-Nine:
Those Who Are Chosen (2)

Jesus said, "Blessed are those who are One – those who are chosen, because you'll find Ultimate Reality. You've come from there and will return there."

Saying Fifty:
Our Origin and Identity

Jesus said, "If they ask you, 'Where do you come from?' tell them, 'We've come from the light, the place where light came into being by itself, established itself, and appeared in their image.'

"If they ask you, 'Is it you?' then say, 'We are its children, and we're chosen by our living Source.'

"If they ask you, 'What's the sign of your Source in you?' then say, 'It's movement and rest.'"

Saying Fifty-One:
The New World

"When will the dead have rest," his disciples asked him, "and when will the new world come?"

"What you're looking for has already come; but you," he told them, "you don't know it."

Saying Fifty-Two:
Twenty-Four Prophets

"Twenty-four prophets have spoken in Israel," his disciples told him, "and they all spoke of you."

"You've ignored the Living One right in front of you," he told them, "and you've talked about those who are dead."

Saying Fifty-Three:
True Circumcision

His disciples asked him, "Is circumcision useful, or not?"

"If it were useful," he told them, "parents would have children who are born circumcised. But the true circumcision in spirit has become profitable in every way."

Saying Fifty-Four:
Those Who Are Poor

Jesus said, "Blessed are those who are poor, for yours is Ultimate Reality."

Saying Fifty-Five:
Discipleship (1)

Jesus said, "Whoever doesn't disregard their father and mother can't become my disciple, and whoever doesn't disregard their brothers and sisters and take up their cross like I do isn't worthy of me."

Saying Fifty-Six:
The World is a Corpse

Jesus said, "Whoever has known the world has found a corpse. Whoever has found a corpse, of them the world isn't worthy."

Saying Fifty-Seven:
The Parable of the Weeds

Jesus said, "Ultimate Reality can be compared to someone who had good seed. Their enemy came by night and sowed weeds among the good seed. The person didn't let anyone pull out the weeds, 'so that you don't pull out the wheat along with the weeds,' they told them. 'On the day of the harvest, the weeds will be obvious. Then they'll be pulled out and burned.'"

Saying Fifty-Eight:
Finding Life

Jesus said, "Blessed is the person who's gone to a lot of trouble. They've found life."

Saying Fifty-Nine:
The Living One

Jesus said, "Look for the Living One while you're still alive. If you die and then try to look for him, you won't be able to."

Saying Sixty:
Don't Become a Corpse

They saw a Samaritan carrying a lamb to Judea. He asked his disciples, "What do you think he's going to do with that lamb?"

"He's going to kill it and eat it," they told him.

"While it's living," he told them, "he won't eat it, but only after he kills it and it becomes a corpse."

"He can't do it any other way," they said.

"You, too, look for a resting place," he told them, "so that you won't become a corpse and be eaten."

Saying Sixty-One:
Jesus and Salome

Jesus said, "Two will rest on a couch. One will die, the other will live."

"Who do you think you are," Salome asked, "to climb onto my couch and eat off my table as if you're from someone?"

"I'm the one who exists in equality," Jesus told her. "Some of what belongs to my Source was given to me."

"I'm your disciple."

"So I'm telling you, if someone is equal, they'll be full of light; but if they're divided, they'll be full of darkness."

Saying Sixty-Two:
Mysteries

Jesus said, "I tell my mysteries to those who are worthy of my mysteries. Don't let your left hand know what your right hand is doing."

Saying Sixty-Three:
The Parable of the Rich Fool

Jesus said, "There was a rich man who had much money. He said, 'I'll use my money to sow, reap, plant, and fill my barns with fruit, so that I won't need anything.' That's what he was thinking to himself, but he died that very night. Anyone who has ears to hear should hear!"

Saying Sixty-Four:
The Parable of the Dinner Party

Jesus said, "Someone was planning on having guests. When dinner was ready, they sent their servant to call the visitors.

"The servant went to the first and said, 'My master invites you.'

"They replied, 'Some merchants owe me money. They're coming tonight. I need to go and give them instructions. Excuse me from the dinner.'

"The servant went to another one and said, 'My master invites you.'

"They replied, "I've just bought a house and am needed for the day. I won't have time.'

"The servant went to another one and said, 'My master invites you.'

"They replied, 'My friend is getting married and I'm going to make dinner. I can't come. Excuse me from the dinner.'

"The servant went to another one and said, 'My master invites you.'

"They replied, "I've just bought a farm and am going to collect the rent. I can't come. Excuse me.'

"The servant went back and told the master, 'The ones you've invited to the dinner have excused themselves.'

"The master said to their servant, 'Go out to the roads and bring whomever you find so that they can have dinner.'

"Those who are consumed with buying and selling won't enter Ultimate Reality."

Saying Sixty-Five:
The Parable of the Sharecroppers

He said, "A creditor owned a vineyard. He leased it out to some sharecroppers to work it so he could collect its fruit.

"He sent his servant so that the sharecroppers could give him the fruit of the vineyard. They seized his servant, beat him, and nearly killed him.

"The servant went back and told his master. His master said, 'Maybe he just didn't know them.' He sent another servant, but the tenants beat that one too.

"Then the master sent his son, thinking, 'Maybe they'll show some respect to my son.'

"Because they knew that he was the heir of the vineyard, the sharecroppers seized and killed him. Anyone who has ears to hear should hear!"

Saying Sixty-Six:
The Rejected Cornerstone

Jesus said, "Show me the stone the builders rejected; that's the cornerstone."

Saying Sixty-Seven:
Knowing Isn't Everything

Jesus said, "Whoever knows everything, but is personally lacking, lacks everything."

Saying Sixty-Eight:
Harassment

Jesus said, "Blessed are you when you're hated and harassed, and no place will be found where you've been harassed."

Saying Sixty-Nine:
Those Who Are Harassed

Jesus said, "Blessed are those who've been harassed in their own hearts. They've truly known the Source. Blessed are those who are hungry, so that their stomachs may be filled."

Saying Seventy:
Salvation is Within

Jesus said, "If you give birth to what's within you, what you have within you will save you. If you don't have that within you, what you don't have within you will kill you."

Saying Seventy-One:
Destroying the Temple

Jesus said, "I'll destroy this house, and no one will be able to rebuild it."

Saying Seventy-Two:
Not a Divider

Someone told him, "Tell my brothers and sisters to divide our inheritance with me."
He asked, "Who made me a divider?"
He turned to his disciples and asked, "Am I really a divider?"

Saying Seventy-Three:
Workers for the Harvest

Jesus said, "The harvest really is plentiful, but the workers are few. So pray that the Lord will send workers to the harvest."

Saying Seventy-Four:
The Empty Well

He said, "Lord, many are gathered around the well, but there's nothing to drink."

Saying Seventy-Five:
The Bridal Chamber

Jesus said, "Many are waiting at the door, but those who are One will enter the bridal chamber."

Saying Seventy-Six:
The Parable of the Pearl

Jesus said, "Ultimate Reality can be compared to a merchant with merchandise who found a pearl. The merchant was wise; they sold their merchandise and bought that single pearl for themselves.

"You, too, look for the treasure that doesn't perish but endures, where no moths come to eat and no worms destroy."

Saying Seventy-Seven:
Jesus is Everything

Jesus said, "I'm the light that's over everything. I am everything; it's come from me and unfolds toward me.

"Split a log; I'm there. Lift the stone, and you'll find me there."

Saying Seventy-Eight:
Into the Desert

Jesus said, "What did you go out into the desert to see? A reed shaken by the wind? A person wearing fancy clothes, like your rulers and powerful people? They wear fancy clothes, but can't know the truth."

Saying Seventy-Nine:
Listening to the Message

A woman in the crowd told him, "Blessed is the womb that bore you, and the breasts that nourished you."

He told her, "Blessed are those who have listened to the message of the Source and kept it, because there will be days when you'll say, 'Blessed is the womb that didn't conceive and the breasts that haven't given milk.'"

Saying Eighty:
The World is a Body

Jesus said, "Whoever has known the world has found the body; but whoever has found the body, of them the world isn't worthy."

Saying Eighty-One:
Riches and Renunciation (1)

Jesus said, "Whoever has become rich should become a ruler, and whoever has power should renounce it."

Saying Eighty-Two:
Jesus and Fire (2)

Jesus said, "Whoever is near me is near the fire, and whoever is far from me is far from Ultimate Reality."

Saying Eighty-Three:
Light and Images

Jesus said, "Images are revealed to people, but the light within them is hidden in the image of the Source's light. It'll be revealed, but its image will be hidden by its light."

Saying Eighty-Four:
Our Previous Images

Jesus said, "When you see your likeness, you rejoice. But when you see your images that came into being before you did – which don't die, and aren't revealed – how much you'll have to bear!"

Saying Eighty-Five:
Adam Wasn't Worthy

Jesus said, "Adam came into being from a great power and great wealth, but he didn't become worthy of you. If he had been worthy, he wouldn't have tasted death."

Saying Eighty-Six:
Foxes and Birds

Jesus said, "The foxes have dens and the birds have nests, but the Son of Humanity has nowhere to lay his head and rest."

Saying Eighty-Seven:
Body and Soul

Jesus said, "How miserable is the body that depends on a body, and how miserable is the soul that depends on both."

Saying Eighty-Eight:
Angels and Prophets

Jesus said, "The angels and the prophets will come to you and give you what belongs to you. You'll give them what you have and ask yourselves, 'When will they come and take what is theirs?'"

Saying Eighty-Nine:
Inside and Outside

Jesus asked, "Why do you wash the outside of the cup? Don't you know that whoever created the inside created the outside too?"

Saying Ninety:
Jesus' Work is Easy

Jesus said, "Come to me, because my work is easy and my requirements are light. You'll be refreshed."

Saying Ninety-One:
Reading the Signs

They told him, "Tell us who you are so that we may trust you."
He told them, "You read the face of the sky and the earth, but you don't know the one right in front of you, and you don't know how to read the present moment."

Saying Ninety-Two:
Look and Find

Jesus said, "Look and you'll find. I didn't answer your questions before. Now I want to give you answers, but you aren't looking for them."

Saying Ninety-Three:
Don't Throw Pearls to Pigs

"Don't give what's holy to the dogs, or else it might be thrown on the manure pile. Don't throw pearls to the pigs, or else they might trample them."

Saying Ninety-Four:
Knock and It Will Be Opened

Jesus said, "Whoever looks will find, and whoever knocks, it will be opened for them."

Saying Ninety-Five:
Giving Money

Jesus said, "If you have money, don't lend it at interest. Instead, give it to someone from whom you won't get it back."

Saying Ninety-Six:
The Parable of the Yeast

Jesus said, "Ultimate Reality can be compared to a woman who took a little yeast and hid it in flour. She made it into large loaves of bread. Anyone who has ears to hear should hear!"

Saying Ninety-Seven:
The Parable of the Jar of Flour

Jesus said, "Ultimate Reality can be compared to a woman carrying a jar of flour. While she was walking down a long road, the jar's handle broke and the flour spilled out behind her on the road. She didn't know it, and didn't realize there was a problem until she got home, put down the jar, and found it empty."

Saying Ninety-Eight:
The Parable of the Assassin

Jesus said, "Ultimate Reality can be compared to a man who wanted to kill someone powerful. He drew his sword in his house and drove it into the wall to figure out whether his hand was strong enough. Then he killed the powerful one."

Saying Ninety-Nine:
Jesus' True Family

The disciples told him, "Your brothers and sisters and mother are standing outside."

He told them, "The people here who live in harmony with my Source are my brothers and sister and mother; they're the ones who will enter Ultimate Reality."

Saying One Hundred:
Give to Caesar What Belongs to Caesar

They showed Jesus a gold coin and told him, "Those who belong to Caesar demand tribute from us."

He told them, "Give to Caesar what belongs to Caesar, give to God what belongs to God, and give to me what belongs to me."

Saying One Hundred and One:
Discipleship (2)

"Whoever doesn't disregard their father and mother as I do can't become my disciple, and whoever doesn't love their father and mother as I do can't become my disciple. For my mother gave birth to my body, but my true Mother gave me Life."

Saying One Hundred and Two:
The Dog in the Feeding Trough

Jesus said, "How awful for the Pharisees who are like a dog sleeping in a feeding trough for cattle, because the dog doesn't eat, and doesn't let the cattle eat either."

Saying One Hundred and Three:
The Parable of the Bandits

Jesus said, "Blessed is the one who knows where the bandits are going to enter. They can get up to assemble their defenses and be prepared to defend themselves before they arrive."

Saying One Hundred and Four:
Prayer and Fasting

They told Jesus, "Come, let's pray and fast today."
Jesus asked, "What have I done wrong? Have I failed?
"Rather, when the groom leaves the bridal chamber, then people should fast and pray."

Saying One Hundred and Five:
Knowing Father and Mother

Jesus said, "Whoever knows their father and mother will be vilified."

Saying One Hundred and Six:
Unity (2)

Jesus said, "When you make the two into One, you'll become Children of Humanity, and if you say 'Mountain, go away!', it'll go."

Saying One Hundred and Seven:
The Parable of the Lost Sheep

Jesus said, "Ultimate Reality can be compared to a shepherd who had a hundred sheep. The largest one strayed. He left the ninety-nine and looked for that one until he found it. Having gone through the trouble, he said to the sheep: 'I love you more than the ninety-nine.'"

Saying One Hundred and Eight:
Becoming Like Jesus

Jesus said, "Whoever drinks from my mouth will become like me, and I myself will become like them; then, what's hidden will be revealed to them."

Saying One Hundred and Nine:
The Parable of the Hidden Treasure

Jesus said, "Ultimate Reality can be compared to someone who had a treasure hidden in their field. They didn't know about it. After they died, they left it to their son. The son didn't know it either. He took the field and sold it.

"The buyer plowed the field, found the treasure, and began to loan money at interest to whomever they wanted."

Saying One Hundred and Ten:
Riches and Renunciation (2)

Jesus said, "Whoever has found the world and become rich should renounce the world."

Saying One Hundred and Eleven:
Those Who Are Living Won't Die (2)

Jesus said, "The heavens and the earth will roll up in front of you, and whoever lives from the Living One won't see death."

Doesn't Jesus say, "Whoever finds themselves, of them the world isn't worthy"?

Saying One Hundred and Twelve:
Flesh and Soul

Jesus said, "How awful for the flesh that depends on the soul. How awful for the soul that depends on the flesh."

Saying One Hundred and Thirteen:
Ultimate Reality is Already Present

His disciples asked him, "When will Ultimate Reality arrive?"

"It won't come by looking for it. They won't say, 'Look over here!' or 'Look over there!' Rather, Ultimate Reality is already spread throughout the earth, and people don't see it."

Saying One Hundred and Fourteen:
Peter and Mary

Simon Peter told them, "Mary should leave us, because women aren't worthy of life."

Jesus said, "Look, am I to make her a man? So that she may become a living spirit too, she's equal to you men, because every woman who makes herself courageous will enter Ultimate Reality."

The Gospel
According to Thomas

Appendix
The Gospel of Thomas
A Literal Translation

The translation of Thomas' Gospel presented in this Appendix has been committed to the public domain. It may be freely copied and used, in whole or in part, changed or unchanged, for any purpose.

The text is based on NHC II,*2* – that is, the second tractate of Volume II of the Nag Hammadi Codices, a Coptic library of ancient texts dating to the fourth century. The Nag Hammadi manuscript contains the most complete copy of Thomas' Gospel discovered so far. It's a fourth-century translation of an earlier Greek text.

In addition to the Coptic manuscript, three smaller Greek fragments also came to light in the nineteenth and twentieth centuries. The Greek copies date to the third century, which proves that Thomas' Gospel was widely copied in antiquity.

All four copies were discovered in Egypt. Scholars widely agree that the original Gospel was probably written in the Greek language in Syria in the late first or early second century, meaning it was written at least as early as the latest books of the New Testament.

What follows is a more literal translation than the one in Chapter Four. For a detailed description of the differences between the two, see Chapter Three.

There are some gaps (known as "lacunae") in the manuscript that are denoted in the literal translation by square brackets. Words in square brackets are hypothetical reconstructions (educated guesses) based on the size of the gap, the number of letters that probably would have fit in that gap, and the surrounding context. Angled brackets denote an emendation or correction of what appears to be a scribal error, and words in parentheses are strictly editorial additions to clarify the meaning of the text. Finally, the labels of the sayings are not in the original Coptic, but are provided for ease of reference.

Incipit

These are the hidden sayings that the living Jesus spoke and Didymos Judas Thomas wrote down.

Saying One:
True Meaning

And he said, "Whoever discovers the meaning of these sayings won't taste death."

Saying Two:
Seek and Find

Jesus said, "Whoever seeks shouldn't stop until they find. When they find, they'll be disturbed. When they're disturbed, they'll be […] amazed, and reign over the All."

Saying Three:
Seeking Within

Jesus said, "If your leaders tell you, 'Look, the kingdom is in heaven,' then the birds of heaven will precede you. If they tell you, 'It's in the sea,' then the fish will precede you. Rather, the kingdom is within you and outside of you.

"When you know yourselves, then you'll be known, and you'll realize that you're the children of the living Father. But if you don't know yourselves, then you live in poverty, and you are the poverty."

Saying Four:
First and Last

Jesus said, "The older person won't hesitate to ask a little seven-day-old child about the place of life, and they'll live, because many who are first will be last, and they'll become one."

Saying Five:
Hidden and Revealed

Jesus said, "Know what's in front of your face, and what's hidden from you will be revealed to you, because there's nothing hidden that won't be revealed."

Saying Six:
Public Ritual

His disciples said to him, "Do you want us to fast? And how should we pray? Should we make donations? And what food should we avoid?"

Jesus said, "Don't lie, and don't do what you hate, because everything is revealed in the sight of heaven; for there's nothing hidden that won't be revealed, and nothing covered up that will stay secret."

Saying Seven:
The Lion and the Human

Jesus said, "Blessed is the lion that's eaten by a human and then becomes human, but how awful for the human who's eaten by a lion, and the lion becomes human."

Saying Eight:
The Parable of the Fish

He said, "The human being is like a wise fisher who cast a net into the sea and drew it up from the sea full of little fish. Among them the wise fisher found a fine large fish and cast all the little fish back down into the sea, easily choosing the large fish. Anyone who has ears to hear should hear!"

Saying Nine:
The Parable of the Sower

Jesus said, "Look, a sower went out, took a handful of seeds, and scattered them. Some fell on the roadside; the birds came and gathered them. Others fell on the rock; they didn't take root in the soil and ears of grain didn't rise toward heaven. Yet others fell on thorns; they choked the seeds and worms ate them. Finally, others fell on good soil; it produced fruit up toward heaven, some sixty times as much and some a hundred and twenty."

Saying Ten:
Jesus and Fire (1)

Jesus said, "I've cast fire on the world, and look, I'm watching over it until it blazes."

Saying Eleven:
Those Who Are Living Won't Die (1)

Jesus said, "This heaven will disappear, and the one above it will disappear too. Those who are dead aren't alive, and those who are living won't die. In the days when you ate what was dead, you made it alive. When you're in the light, what will you do? On the day when you were one, you became divided. But when you become divided, what will you do?"

Saying Twelve:
James the Just

The disciples said to Jesus, "We know you're going to leave us. Who will lead us then?"

Jesus said to them, "Wherever you are, you'll go to James the Just, for whom heaven and earth came into being."

Saying Thirteen:
Thomas' Confession

Jesus said to his disciples, "If you were to compare me to someone, who would you say I'm like?"

Simon Peter said to him, "You're like a just angel."

Matthew said to him, "You're like a wise philosopher."

Thomas said to him, "Teacher, I'm completely unable to say whom you're like."

Jesus said, "I'm not your teacher. Because you've drunk, you've become intoxicated by the bubbling spring I've measured out."

He took him aside and told him three things. When Thomas returned to his companions, they asked, "What did Jesus say to you?"

Thomas said to them, "If I tell you one of the things he said to me, you'll pick up stones and cast them at me, and fire will come out of the stones and burn you up."

Saying Fourteen:
Public Ministry

Jesus said to them, "If you fast, you'll bring guilt upon yourselves; and if you pray, you'll be condemned; and if you make donations, you'll harm your spirits.

"If they welcome you when you enter any land and go around in the countryside, heal those who are sick among them and eat whatever they give you, because it's not what goes into your mouth that will defile you. What comes out of your mouth is what will defile you."

Saying Fifteen:
Worship

Jesus said, "When you see the one who wasn't born of a woman, fall down on your face and worship that person. That's your Father."

Saying Sixteen:
Not Peace, but War

Jesus said, "Maybe people think that I've come to cast peace on the world, and they don't know that I've come to cast divisions on the earth: fire, sword, and war. Where there are five in a house, there'll be three against two and two against three, father against and son and son against father. They'll stand up and be one."

Saying Seventeen:
Divine Gift

Jesus said, "I'll give you what no eye has ever seen, no ear has ever heard, no hand has ever touched, and no human mind has ever thought."

Saying Eighteen:
Beginning and End

The disciples said to Jesus, "Tell us about our end. How will it come?"
Jesus said, "Have you discovered the beginning so that you can look for the end? Because the end will be where the beginning is. Blessed is the one who will stand up in the beginning. They'll know the end, and won't taste death."

Saying Nineteen:
Five Trees in Paradise

Jesus said, "Blessed is the one who came into being before coming into being. If you become my disciples and listen to my message, these stones will become your servants; because there are five trees in paradise which don't change in summer or winter, and their leaves don't fall. Whoever knows them won't taste death."

Saying Twenty:
The Parable of the Mustard Seed

The disciples asked Jesus, "Tell us, what can the kingdom of heaven be compared to?"

He said to them, "It can be compared to a mustard seed. Though it's the smallest of all the seeds, when it falls on tilled soil it makes a plant so large that it shelters the birds of heaven."

Saying Twenty-One:
The Parables of the Field, the Bandits, and the Reaper

Mary said to Jesus, "Whom are your disciples like?"

He said, "They're like little children living in a field which isn't theirs. When the owners of the field come, they'll say, 'Give our field back to us.' They'll strip naked in front of them to let them have it and give them their field.

"So I say that if the owner of the house realizes the bandit is coming, they'll watch out beforehand and won't let the bandit break into the house of their domain and steal their possessions. You, then, watch out for the world! Prepare to defend yourself so that the bandits don't attack you, because what you're expecting will come. May there be a wise person among you!

"When the fruit ripened, the reaper came quickly, sickle in hand, and harvested it. Anyone who has ears to hear should hear!"

Saying Twenty-Two:
Making the Two into One

Jesus saw some little children nursing. He said to his disciples, "These nursing children can be compared to those who enter the kingdom."

They said to him, "Then we'll enter the kingdom as little children?"

Jesus said to them, "When you make the two into one, and make the inner like the outer and the outer like the inner, and the upper like the lower, and so make the male and the female a single one so that the male won't be male nor the female female; when you make eyes in the place of an eye, a hand in the place of a hand, a foot in the place of a foot, and an image in the place of an image; then you'll enter [the kingdom]."

Saying Twenty-Three:
Those Who are Chosen (1)

Jesus said, "I'll choose you, one out of a thousand and two out of ten thousand, and they'll stand as a single one."

Saying Twenty-Four:
Light

His disciples said, "Show us the place where you are, because we need to look for it."

He said to them, "Anyone who has ears to hear should hear! Light exists within a person of light, and they light up the whole world. If they don't shine, there's darkness."

Saying Twenty-Five:
Love and Protect

Jesus said, "Love your brother as your own soul. Protect them like the pupil of your eye."

Saying Twenty-Six:
Speck and Beam

Jesus said, "You see the speck that's in your brother's eye, but you don't see the beam in your own eye. When you get the beam out of your own eye, then you'll be able to see clearly to get the speck out of your brother's eye."

Saying Twenty-Seven:
Fasting and Sabbath

"If you don't fast from the world, you won't find the kingdom. If you don't make the Sabbath into a Sabbath, you won't see the Father."

Saying Twenty-Eight:
The World is Drunk

Jesus said, "I stood in the middle of the world and appeared to them in the flesh. I found them all drunk; I didn't find any of them thirsty. My soul ached for the children of humanity, because they were blind in their hearts and couldn't see. They came into the world empty and plan on leaving the world empty. Meanwhile, they're drunk. When they shake off their wine, then they'll change."

Saying Twenty-Nine:
Spirit and Body

Jesus said, "If the flesh came into existence because of spirit, that's amazing. If spirit came into existence because of the body, that's really amazing! But I'm amazed at how [such] great wealth has been placed in this poverty."

Saying Thirty:
Divine Presence

Jesus said, "Where there are three deities, they're divine. Where there are two or one, I'm with them."

Saying Thirty-One:
Prophet and Doctor

Jesus said, "No prophet is welcome in their own village. No doctor heals those who know them."

Saying Thirty-Two:
The Parable of the Fortified City

Jesus said, "A city built and fortified on a high mountain can't fall, nor can it be hidden."

Saying Thirty-Three:
The Parable of the Lamp

Jesus said, "What you hear with one ear, listen to with both, then proclaim from your rooftops. No one lights a lamp and puts it under a basket or in a hidden place. Rather, they put it on the stand so that everyone who comes and goes can see its light."

Saying Thirty-Four:
The Parable of Those Who Can't See

Jesus said, "If someone who's blind leads someone else who's blind, both of them fall into a pit."

Saying Thirty-Five:
The Parable of Binding the Strong

Jesus said, "No one can break into the house of the strong and take it by force without tying the hands of the strong. Then they can loot the house."

Saying Thirty-Six:
Anxiety

Jesus said, "Don't be anxious from morning to evening or from evening to morning about what you'll wear."

Saying Thirty-Seven:
Seeing Jesus

His disciples said, "When will you appear to us? When will we see you?"
Jesus said, "When you strip naked without being ashamed, and throw your clothes on the ground and stomp on them as little children would, then [you'll] see the Son of the Living One and won't be afraid."

Saying Thirty-Eight:
Finding Jesus

Jesus said, "Often you've wanted to hear this message that I'm telling you, and you don't have anyone else from whom to hear it. There will be days when you'll look for me, but you won't be able to find me."

Saying Thirty-Nine:
The Keys of Knowledge

Jesus said, "The Pharisees and the scholars have taken the keys of knowledge and hidden them. They haven't entered, and haven't let others enter who wanted to. So be wise as serpents and innocent as doves."

Saying Forty:
A Grapevine

Jesus said, "A grapevine has been planted outside of the Father. Since it's malnourished, it'll be pulled up by its root and destroyed."

Saying Forty-One:
More and Less

Jesus said, "Whoever has something in hand will be given more, but whoever doesn't have anything will lose even what little they do have."

Saying Forty-Two:
Passing By

Jesus said, "Become passersby."

Saying Forty-Three:
The Tree and the Fruit

His disciples said to him, "Who are you to say these things to us?"

"You don't realize who I am from what I say to you, but you've become like those Judeans who either love the tree but hate its fruit, or love the fruit but hate the tree."

Saying Forty-Four:
Blasphemy

Jesus said, "Whoever blasphemes the Father will be forgiven, and whoever blasphemes the Son will be forgiven, but whoever blasphemes the Holy Spirit will not be forgiven, neither on earth nor in heaven."

Saying Forty-Five:
Good and Evil

Jesus said, "Grapes aren't harvested from thorns, nor are figs gathered from thistles, because they don't produce fruit. [A person who's good] brings good things out of their treasure, and a person who's [evil] brings evil things out of their evil treasure. They say evil things because their heart is full of evil."

Saying Forty-Six:
Greater than John the Baptizer

Jesus said, "From Adam to John the Baptizer, no one's been born who's so much greater than John the Baptizer that they shouldn't avert their eyes. But I say that whoever among you will become a little child will know the kingdom and become greater than John."

Saying Forty-Seven:
The Parables of Divided Loyalties, New Wine in Old Wineskins, and New Patch on Old Cloth

Jesus said, "It's not possible for anyone to mount two horses or stretch two bows, and it's not possible for a servant to follow two leaders, because they'll respect one and despise the other.

"No one drinks old wine and immediately wants to drink new wine. And new wine isn't put in old wineskins, because they'd burst. Nor is old wine put in new wineskins, because it'd spoil.

"A new patch of cloth isn't sewn onto an old coat, because it'd tear apart."

Saying Forty-Eight:
Unity (1)

Jesus said, "If two make peace with each other in a single house, they'll say to the mountain, 'Go away,' and it will."

Saying Forty-Nine:
Those Who Are Chosen (2)

Jesus said, "Blessed are those who are one – those who are chosen, because you'll find the kingdom. You've come from there and will return there."

Saying Fifty:
Our Origin and Identity

Jesus said, "If they ask you, 'Where do you come from?' tell them, 'We've come from the light, the place where light came into being by itself, [established] itself, and appeared in their image.'

"If they ask you, 'Is it you?' then say, 'We are its children, and we're chosen by our living Father.'

"If they ask you, 'What's the sign of your Father in you?' then say, 'It's movement and rest.'"

Saying Fifty-One:
The New World

His disciples said to him, "When will the dead have rest, and when will the new world come?"

He said to them, "What you're looking for has already come, but you don't know it."

Saying Fifty-Two:
Twenty-Four Prophets

His disciples said to him, "Twenty-four prophets have spoken in Israel, and they all spoke of you."

He said to them, "You've ignored the Living One right in front of you, and you've talked about those who are dead."

Saying Fifty-Three:
True Circumcision

His disciples said to him, "Is circumcision useful, or not?"

He said to them, "If it were useful, parents would have children who are born circumcised. But the true circumcision in spirit has become profitable in every way."

Saying Fifty-Four:
Those Who Are Poor

Jesus said, "Blessed are those who are poor, for yours is the kingdom of heaven."

Saying Fifty-Five:
Discipleship (1)

Jesus said, "Whoever doesn't hate their father and mother can't become my disciple, and whoever doesn't hate their brothers and sisters and take up their cross like I do isn't worthy of me."

Saying Fifty-Six:
The World is a Corpse

Jesus said, "Whoever has known the world has found a corpse. Whoever has found a corpse, of them the world isn't worthy."

Saying Fifty-Seven:
The Parable of the Weeds

Jesus said, "My Fathers' kingdom can be compared to someone who had [good] seed. Their enemy came by night and sowed weeds among the good seed. The person didn't let anyone pull out the weeds, 'so that you don't pull out the wheat along with the weeds,' they said to them. 'On the day of the harvest, the weeds will be obvious. Then they'll be pulled out and burned.'"

Saying Fifty-Eight:
Finding Life

Jesus said, "Blessed is the person who's gone to a lot of trouble. They've found life."

Saying Fifty-Nine:
The Living One

Jesus said, "Look for the Living One while you're still alive. If you die and then try to look for him, you won't be able to."

Saying Sixty:
Don't Become a Corpse

They saw a Samaritan carrying a lamb to Judea. He said to his disciples, "What do you think he's going to do with that lamb?"

They said to him, "He's going to kill it and eat it."

He said to them, "While it's living, he won't eat it, but only after he kills it and it becomes a corpse."

They said, "He can't do it any other way."

He said to them, "You, too, look for a resting place, so that you won't become a corpse and be eaten."

Saying Sixty-One:
Jesus and Salome

Jesus said, "Two will rest on a couch. One will die, the other will live."

Salome said, "Who are you, Sir, to climb onto my couch and eat off my table as if you're from someone?"

Jesus said to her, "I'm the one who exists in equality. Some of what belongs to my Father was given to me."

"I'm your disciple."

"So I'm telling you, if someone is <equal>, they'll be full of light; but if they're divided, they'll be full of darkness."

Saying Sixty-Two:
Mysteries

Jesus said, "I tell my mysteries to [those who are worthy of my] mysteries. Don't let your left hand know what your right hand is doing."

Saying Sixty-Three:
The Parable of the Rich Fool

Jesus said, "There was a rich man who had much money. He said, 'I'll use my money to sow, reap, plant, and fill my barns with fruit, so that I won't need anything.' That's what he was thinking to himself, but he died that very night. Anyone who has ears to hear should hear!"

Saying Sixty-Four:
The Parable of the Dinner Party

Jesus said, "Someone was planning on having guests. When dinner was ready, they sent their servant to call the visitors.

"The servant went to the first and said, 'My master invites you.'

"They said, 'Some merchants owe me money. They're coming tonight. I need to go and give them instructions. Excuse me from the dinner.'

"The servant went to another one and said, 'My master invites you.'

"They said, "I've just bought a house and am needed for the day. I won't have time.'

"The servant went to another one and said, 'My master invites you.'

"They said, 'My friend is getting married and I'm going to make dinner. I can't come. Excuse me from the dinner.'

"The servant went to another one and said, 'My master invites you.'

"They said, "I've just bought a farm and am going to collect the rent. I can't come. Excuse me.'

"The servant went back and told the master, 'The ones you've invited to the dinner have excused themselves.'

"The master said to their servant, 'Go out to the roads and bring whomever you find so that they can have dinner.'

"Buyers and merchants won't [enter] the places of my Father."

Saying Sixty-Five:
The Parable of the Sharecroppers

He said, "A [creditor] owned a vineyard. He leased it out to some sharecroppers to work it so he could collect its fruit.

"He sent his servant so that the sharecroppers could give him the fruit of the vineyard. They seized his servant, beat him, and nearly killed him.

"The servant went back and told his master. His master said, 'Maybe he just didn't know them.' He sent another servant, but the tenants beat that one too.

"Then the master sent his son, thinking, 'Maybe they'll show some respect to my son.'

"Because they knew that he was the heir of the vineyard, the sharecroppers seized and killed him. Anyone who has ears to hear should hear!"

Saying Sixty-Six:
The Rejected Cornerstone

Jesus said, "Show me the stone the builders rejected; that's the cornerstone."

Saying Sixty-Seven:
Knowing Isn't Everything

Jesus said, "Whoever knows everything, but is personally lacking, lacks everything."

Saying Sixty-Eight:
Persecution

Jesus said, "Blessed are you when you're hated and persecuted, and no place will be found where you've been persecuted."

Saying Sixty-Nine:
Those Who Are Persecuted

Jesus said, "Blessed are those who've been persecuted in their own hearts. They've truly known the Father. Blessed are those who are hungry, so that their stomachs may be filled."

Saying Seventy:
Salvation is Within

Jesus said, "If you give birth to what's within you, what you have within you will save you. If you don't have that within [you], what you don't have within you [will] kill you."

Saying Seventy-One:
Destroying the Temple

Jesus said, "I'll destroy [this] house, and no one will be able to build it [...]"

Saying Seventy-Two:
Not a Divider

[Someone said to him], "Tell my brothers to divide our inheritance with me."

He said to him, "Who made me a divider?"

He turned to his disciples and said to them, "Am I really a divider?"

Saying Seventy-Three:
Workers for the Harvest

Jesus said, "The harvest really is plentiful, but the workers are few. So pray that the Lord will send workers to the harvest."

Saying Seventy-Four:
The Empty Well

He said, "Lord, many are gathered around the well, but there's nothing to drink."

Saying Seventy-Five:
The Bridal Chamber

Jesus said, "Many are waiting at the door, but those who are one will enter the bridal chamber."

Saying Seventy-Six:
The Parable of the Pearl

Jesus said, "The Father's kingdom can be compared to a merchant with merchandise who found a pearl. The merchant was wise; they sold their merchandise and bought that single pearl for themselves.

"You, too, look for the treasure that doesn't perish but endures, where no moths come to eat and no worms destroy."

Saying Seventy-Seven:
Jesus is the All

Jesus said, "I'm the light that's over all. I am the All. The All has come from me and unfolds toward me.

"Split a log; I'm there. Lift the stone, and you'll find me there."

Saying Seventy-Eight:
Into the Desert

Jesus said, "What did you go out into the desert to see? A reed shaken by the wind? A [person] wearing fancy clothes, [like your] rulers and powerful people? They (wear) fancy [clothes], but can't know the truth."

Saying Seventy-Nine:
Listening to the Message

A woman in the crowd said to him, "Blessed is the womb that bore you, and the breasts that nourished you."

He said to [her], "Blessed are those who have listened to the message of the Father and kept it, because there will be days when you'll say, 'Blessed is the womb that didn't conceive and the breasts that haven't given milk.'"

Saying Eighty:
The World is a Body

Jesus said, "Whoever has known the world has found the body; but whoever has found the body, of them the world isn't worthy."

Saying Eighty-One:
Riches and Renunciation (1)

Jesus said, "Whoever has become rich should become a ruler, and whoever has power should renounce it."

Saying Eighty-Two:
Jesus and Fire (2)

Jesus said, "Whoever is near me is near the fire, and whoever is far from me is far from the kingdom."

Saying Eighty-Three:
Light and Images

Jesus said, "Images are revealed to people, but the light within them is hidden in the image of the Father's light. He'll be revealed, but his image will be hidden by his light."

Saying Eighty-Four:
Our Previous Images

Jesus said, "When you see your likeness, you rejoice. But when you see your images that came into being before you did – which don't die, and aren't revealed – how much you'll have to bear!"

Saying Eighty-Five:
Adam Wasn't Worthy

Jesus said, "Adam came into being from a great power and great wealth, but he didn't become worthy of you. If he had been worthy, [he wouldn't have tasted] death."

Saying Eighty-Six:
Foxes and Birds

Jesus said, "[The foxes have dens] and the birds have nests, but the Son of Humanity has nowhere to lay his head and rest."

Saying Eighty-Seven:
Body and Soul

Jesus said, "How miserable is the body that depends on a body, and how miserable is the soul that depends on both."

Saying Eighty-Eight:
Angels and Prophets

Jesus said, "The angels and the prophets will come to you and give you what belongs to you. You'll give them what you have and ask yourselves, 'When will they come and take what is theirs?'"

Saying Eighty-Nine:
Inside and Outside

Jesus said, "Why do you wash the outside of the cup? Don't you know that whoever created the inside created the outside too?"

Saying Ninety:
Jesus' Yoke is Easy

Jesus said, "Come to me, because my yoke is easy and my requirements are light. You'll be refreshed."

Saying Ninety-One:
Reading the Signs

They said to him, "Tell us who you are so that we may trust you."

He said to them, "You read the face of the sky and the earth, but you don't know the one right in front of you, and you don't know how to read the present moment."

Saying Ninety-Two:
Look and Find

Jesus said, "Look and you'll find. I didn't answer your questions before. Now I want to give you answers, but you aren't looking for them."

Saying Ninety-Three:
Don't Throw Pearls to Pigs

"Don't give what's holy to the dogs, or else it might be thrown on the manure pile. Don't throw pearls to the pigs, or else they might [...]"

Saying Ninety-Four:
Knock and It Will Be Opened

Jesus [said], "Whoever looks will find, [and whoever knocks], it will be opened for them."

Saying Ninety-Five:
Giving Money

[Jesus said], "If you have money, don't lend it at interest. Instead, give [it to] someone from whom you won't get it back."

Saying Ninety-Six:
The Parable of the Yeast

Jesus [said], "The Father's kingdom can be compared to a woman who took a little yeast and [hid] it in flour. She made it into large loaves of bread. Anyone who has ears to hear should hear!"

Saying Ninety-Seven:
The Parable of the Jar of Flour

Jesus said, "The Father's kingdom can be compared to a woman carrying a jar of flour. While she was walking down [a] long road, the jar's handle broke and the flour spilled out behind her on the road. She didn't know it, and didn't realize there was a problem until she got home, put down the jar, and found it empty."

Saying Ninety-Eight:
The Parable of the Assassin

Jesus said, "The Father's kingdom can be compared to a man who wanted to kill someone powerful. He drew his sword in his house and drove it into the wall to figure out whether his hand was strong enough. Then he killed the powerful one."

Saying Ninety-Nine:
Jesus' True Family

The disciples said to him, "Your brothers and mother are standing outside."

He said to them, "The people here who do the will of my Father are my brothers and mother; they're the ones who will enter my Father's kingdom."

Saying One Hundred:
Give to Caesar What Belongs to Caesar

They showed Jesus a gold coin and said to him, "Those who belong to Caesar demand tribute from us."

He said to them, "Give to Caesar what belongs to Caesar, give to God what belongs to God, and give to me what belongs to me."

Saying One Hundred and One:
Discipleship (2)

"Whoever doesn't hate their [father] and mother as I do can't become my [disciple], and whoever [doesn't] love their [father] and mother as I do can't become my [disciple]. For my mother [...], but [my] true [Mother] gave me Life."

Saying One Hundred and Two:
The Dog in the Feeding Trough

Jesus said, "How awful for the Pharisees who are like a dog sleeping in a feeding trough for cattle, because the dog doesn't eat, and [doesn't let] the cattle eat either."

Saying One Hundred and Three:
The Parable of the Bandits

Jesus said, "Blessed is the one who knows where the bandits are going to enter. [They can] get up to assemble their defenses and be prepared to defend themselves before they arrive."

Saying One Hundred and Four:
Prayer and Fasting

They said to [Jesus], "Come, let's pray and fast today."
Jesus said, "What have I done wrong? Have I failed?
"Rather, when the groom leaves the bridal chamber, then people should fast and pray."

Saying One Hundred and Five:
Knowing Father and Mother

Jesus said, "Whoever knows their father and mother will be called a bastard."

Saying One Hundred and Six:
Unity (2)

Jesus said, "When you make the two into one, you'll become Children of Humanity, and if you say 'Mountain, go away!', it'll go."

Saying One Hundred and Seven:
The Parable of the Lost Sheep

Jesus said, "The kingdom can be compared to a shepherd who had a hundred sheep. The largest one strayed. He left the ninety-nine and looked for that one until he found it. Having gone through the trouble, he said to the sheep: 'I love you more than the ninety-nine.'"

Saying One Hundred and Eight:
Becoming Like Jesus

Jesus said, "Whoever drinks from my mouth will become like me, and I myself will become like them; then, what's hidden will be revealed to them."

Saying One Hundred and Nine:
The Parable of the Hidden Treasure

Jesus said, "The kingdom can be compared to someone who had a treasure [hidden] in their field. [They] didn't know about it. After they died, they left it to their son. The son didn't know it either. He took the field and sold it.

"The buyer plowed the field, [found] the treasure, and began to loan money at interest to whomever they wanted."

Saying One Hundred and Ten:
Riches and Renunciation (2)

Jesus said, "Whoever has found the world and become rich should renounce the world."

Saying One Hundred and Eleven:
Those Who are Living Won't Die (2)

Jesus said, "The heavens and the earth will roll up in front of you, and whoever lives from the Living One won't see death."

Doesn't Jesus say, "Whoever finds themselves, of them the world isn't worthy"?

Saying One Hundred and Twelve:
Flesh and Soul

Jesus said, "How awful for the flesh that depends on the soul. How awful for the soul that depends on the flesh."

Saying One Hundred and Thirteen:
The Kingdom is Already Present

His disciples said to him, "When will the kingdom come?"

"It won't come by looking for it. They won't say, 'Look over here!' or 'Look over there!' Rather, the Father's kingdom is already spread out over the earth, and people don't see it."

Saying One Hundred and Fourteen:
Peter and Mary

Simon Peter said to them, "Mary should leave us, because women aren't worthy of life."

Jesus said, "Look, am I to make her a man? So that she may become a living spirit too, she's equal to you men, because every woman who makes herself manly will enter the kingdom of heaven."

The Gospel
According to Thomas

Text Notes

Saying Thirteen

"Three things." Or possibly "three words." The Coptic term for "word" can also be translated as "saying," as in the incipit.

Saying Sixty-One

"Equal." The Coptic literally reads "destroyed," which may be a scribal error; if one letter is changed, the word would be "equal," which would echo the earlier phrase "I am the one who exists in equality."

Saying Sixty-Five

"Creditor." Or possibly "a good person"; cf. Michael W. Grondin, "Good Man or Usurer? Battle over a Lacuna," rev. May 31, 2014, on-line at http://gospel-thomas.net/lacuna.htm. Last accessed August 1, 2015.

Saying One Hundred and Five

"A bastard." Literally, "the son of a prostitute."

Saying One Hundred and Fourteen

"Manly." Cf. the end of Chapter Three.

Notes

Introduction

[1]Bentley Layton, *Coptic in 20 Lessons: Introduction to Sahidic Coptic With Exercises and Vocabularies* (Peeters), 2007, p.1.

[2]Matt. 10:3; Mark 3:18; Luke 6:15; John 11:16; 20:24; cf. Acts 1:13.

[3]Cf. John 11:16; 14:5; 20:24-28.

[4]John 11:16; 20:24; 21:2.

Chapter One

[1]Frequently, this strategy involves identifying Thomas' Gospel as a "Gnostic" text, with "Gnosticism" representing doctrines believed to have been antithetical to genuine Christianity. However, scholars don't agree about what "Gnosticism" was or what "Gnostics" are supposed to have believed, and some have persuasively argued that the category of "Gnosticism" itself is an artificial construct. Cf. Michael Allen Williams, *Rethinking "Gnosticism": An Argument for Dismantling a Dubious Category* (Princeton University Press), 1996, and Karen L. King, *What is Gnosticism?* (Belknap), 2003. See also my book *The Gospel of Judas: The Sarcastic Gospel* (CreateSpace Independent Publishing Platform), 2013, pp. 40-44.

[2]Cf. Marvin Meyer, *The Gospel of Thomas: The Hidden Sayings of Jesus* (HarperSanFrancisco), 1992, p. 111.

[3]Cf. Elaine Pagels, *Beyond Belief: The Secret Gospel of Thomas* (Vintage Books), 2004.

[4]James D.G. Dunn, "The Gospel and the Gospels," *Evangelical Quarterly*, 2013, Vol. 85, No. 4., p. 305.

[5]*Ibid.*, p. 306.

[6]*Ibid.*, p. 307.

[7]Cf. Tom Wright, *The Original Jesus: The Life and Vision of a Revolutionary* (William B. Eerdmans Pub. Co.), 1996, p. 121.

[8]Cf. Dunn, *op. cit.*, p. 305: "Is *Thomas* a 'Gospel'? An immediately obvious answer is 'Yes'."

[9]Wright, *op. cit.*., pp. 126,127.

[10]Wright, *The New Testament and the People of God* (Fortress Press), p. 443.

[11]*Ibid.*, p. 442.

[12]*Ibid.*, p. 214.

[13]Jean-Yves Leloup, *The Gospel of Thomas: The Gnostic Wisdom of Jesus* (Inner Traditions), 2005, pp. 4,5; cp. Leloup, *The Gospel of Philip: Jesus, Mary Magdalene, and the Gnosis of Sacred Union* (Inner Traditions), 2004, p. 2: "It is not my intention to set the canonical and the apocryphal Gospels against each other, nor to privilege one over the others. My aim is to read them together: to hold the manifest together with the hidden, the allowed with the forbidden, the conscious with the unconscious."

[14]Cf. Mark M. Mattison, *The Gospel of Mary: A Fresh Translation and Holistic Approach* (CreateSpace Independent Publishing Platform), 2013, pp. 7-9.

[15]For a more detailed discussion of the "canon" of Scripture see my book *The Gospel of Judas,* pp. 45-48.

Chapter Two

[1]Cf. Robert W. Funk, Roy W. Hoover, and the Jesus Seminar, *The Five Gospels: The Search for the Authentic Words of Jesus* (HarperSanFrancisco), 1993, p. 26.

[2]Cf. Stephen J. Patterson, *The Gospel of Thomas and Jesus* (Polebridge Press), 1993.

Chapter Three

[1]Cf. Robert H. Stein, *The Method and Message of Jesus' Teachings* (The Westminster Press), 1978, pp. 8,9, commenting on the parallel passage in Luke 14:26.

[2]Sayings 15, 27, 40, 44, 50, 61, 69, 79, 83, and 99.

[3]Cf. M. David Litwa, "'I Will Become Him': Homology and Deification in the Gospel of Thomas," *Journal of Biblical Literature,* 2015, Vol. 134, No. 2, p. 446: "Thomas ... appears frankly panentheistic." For an excellent discussion of the merits of panentheism see Elizabeth A. Johnson, *She Who Is: The Mystery of God in Feminist Theological Discourse* (Crossroad), 1992, pp. 230-233.

[4]Revelation 1:17; 2:8; 22:13.

[5]Sayings 3, 20, 22, 27, 46, 49, 54, 57, 64, 76, 82, 96, 97, 98, 99, 107, 109, 113, and 114.

[6]Cf. Sayings 20, 57, 76, 97, 98, 107, and 109.

[7]Cynthia Bourgeault, *The Wisdom Jesus: Transforming Heart and Mind – a New Perspective on Christ and His Message* (Shambhala), 2008, p. 30.

[8]*The Continuing Quest for God: Monastic Spirituality in Tradition and Transition*, ed. William Skudlarek, O.S.B. (The Liturgical Press), 1981, pp. 28,29.

[9]*Ibid.*, p. 28.

[10]Although I haven't capitalized the term "One" in the literal translation.

[11]For more on this, see my book *The Gospel of Mary*, pp. 44,45,49-52.

[12]Samuel Zinner, *The Gospel of Thomas in the Light of Early Jewish, Christian and Islamic Esoteric Trajectories: with a contextualized commentary and a new translation of the Thomas Gospel* (The Matheson Trust), 2011, pp. 288-290.

[13]Paul Schüngel, "Ein Vorschlag, EvTho 114 neu zu übersetzen," *Novum Testamentum*, 1994, Vol. 36, No. 4, pp. 394-401.

[14]Personal correspondence dated January 17, 2015.

Bibliography

Bourgeault, Cynthia, "The Gift of Life: the Unified Solitude of the Desert Fathers," *Parabola*, 1989, Vol. 14, No. 2

Bourgeault, Cynthia, *The Wisdom Jesus: Transforming Heart and Mind – a New Perspective on Christ and His Message* (Shambhala), 2008

Davies, Stevan, *The Gospel of Thomas and Christian Wisdom: Second Edition* (Bardic Press), 2005

Davies, Stevan, *The Gospel of Thomas Annotated & Explained* (Skylight Paths), 2002

Dunn, James D.G., "The Gospel and the Gospels," *Evangelical Quarterly*, 2013, Vol. 85, No. 4., pp. 291-308

Funk, Robert W., Hoover, Roy W., and the Jesus Seminar, *The Five Gospels: The Search for the Authentic Words of Jesus* (HarperSanFrancisco), 1993

Grondin, Michael W., "Good Man or Usurer? Battle over a Lacuna," rev. May 31, 2014, on-line at http://gospel-thomas.net/lacuna.htm. Last accessed August 1, 2015.

Grondin, Michael W., *Grondin's Interlinear Coptic/English Translation of the Gospel of Thomas*, rev. November 22, 2002, on-line at http://gospel-thomas.net/gtbypage_112702.pdf, last accessed August 1, 2015

Johnson, Elizabeth A., *She Who Is: The Mystery of God in Feminist Theological Discourse* (Crossroad), 1992

King, Karen L., *What is Gnosticism?* (Belknap), 2003

Layton, Bentley, *Coptic in 20 Lessons: Introduction to Sahidic Coptic With Exercises and* Vocabularies (Peeters), 2007

Leloup, Jean-Yves, *The Gospel of Philip: Jesus, Mary Magdalene, and the Gnosis of Sacred Union* (Inner Traditions), 2004

Leloup, Jean-Yves, *The Gospel of Thomas: The Gnostic Wisdom of Jesus* (Inner Traditions), 2005

Litwa, M. David, "'I Will Become Him': Homology and Deification in the Gospel of Thomas," *Journal of Biblical Literature*, 2015, Vol. 134, No. 2, pp. 427-447

Mattison, Mark M., *The Gospel of Judas: The Sarcastic Gospel* (CreateSpace Independent Publishing Platform), 2014

Mattison, Mark M., *The Gospel of Mary: A Fresh Translation and Holistic Approach* (CreateSpace Independent Publishing Platform), 2013

Meyer, Marvin, *The Gospel of Thomas: The Hidden Sayings of Jesus* (HarperSanFrancisco), 1992

Miller, Robert J., ed., *The Complete Gospels: Fourth Edition* (Polebridge Press), 2010

Pagels, Elaine, *Beyond Belief: The Secret Gospel of Thomas* (Vintage Books), 2004

Patterson, Stephen J., *The Gospel of Thomas and Jesus* (Polebridge Press), 1993

Stein, Robert H., *The Method and Message of Jesus' Teachings* (The Westminster Press), 1978

Valantasis, Richard, *The Gospel of Thomas* (Routledge), 1997

Williams, Michael Allen, *Rethinking "Gnosticism": An Argument for Dismantling a Dubious Category* (Princeton University Press), 1996

Winkler, Gabriele, "The Origins and Idiosyncrasies of the Earliest Form of Asceticism," *The Continuing Quest for God: Monastic Spirituality in Tradition and Transition*, ed. William Skudlarek, O.S.B. (The Liturgical Press), 1981, pp. 9-41

Wright, N.T., *The Original Jesus: The Life and Vision of a Revolutionary* (William B. Eerdmans Pub. Co.), 1996

Wright, N.T., *The New Testament and the People of God* (Fortress Press), 1992

Zinner, Samuel, *The Gospel of Thomas in the Light of Early Jewish, Christian and Islamic Esoteric Trajectories: with a contextualized commentary and a new translation of the Thomas Gospel* (The Matheson Trust), 2011

Made in the USA
Coppell, TX
27 April 2022

77102210R00052